THIS BOOK BELONG TO

_____

_____

_____

Test Your Colors Here

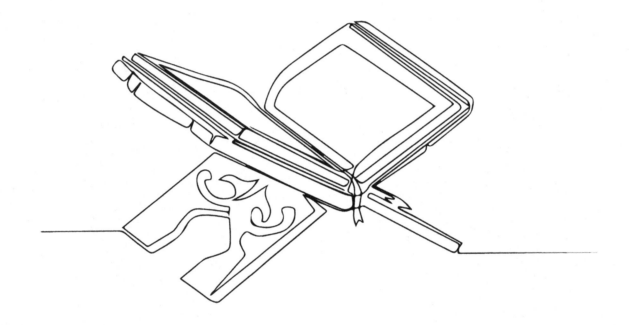

"Call upon me, I will respond to you"

Surah Ghafir 40:60

"And Allah would not punish them while they seek forgiveness"

Surah Al-Anfal 8:33

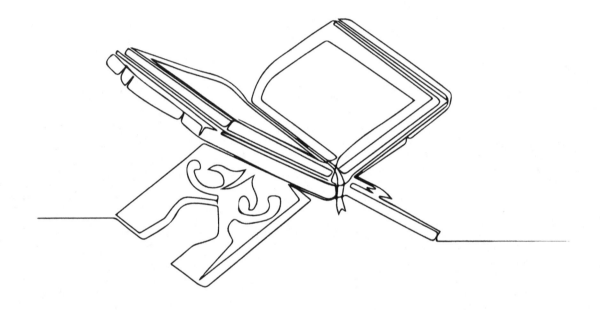

"So remember me; I will remember you"

Surah Al-Baqarah 2:152

"And He has made me blessed wherever I am "

Surah Maryam 19:31

"He knows what is within the heavens and earth and knows what you conceal and what you declare. And Allah (SWT) is Knowing of that within the breasts"

At-Taghabun 64:4

"And whoever puts all his trust in Allah (SWT),
He will be enough for him"

Surah At-Talaq 65:1-3

"Indeed, those who have believed and done righteous deeds will have gardens beneath which rivers flow that is a great attainment"

Surah al-Buruj 85:11

"If you are grateful, I will surely increase you [in favor] "

Surah Ibrahim 14:7

"Between them is a barrier which
they do not transgress"

Surah Al-Rahman

"Do they not see the birds controlled in the atmosphere of the sky?
None holds them up except Allah.
Indeed in that are signs for a people who believe"

Surah An-Nahl (16:79)

"And verily the hereafter, will be better for thee.
Than the present"

Surah Al-Dhuha 93:4

"My mercy embraces all things"

Surat Al-A'raf 7:156

"And who despairs from the mercy of his Lord, except those astray?"

Surah Al-Hijr (15:56)

"You prefer the life of this world,
while the hereafter is better & more lasting"

Surah Al-A'la (87:16)

"My success can only come from Allah"
Surah Hud (11:88)

"Indeed, Allah is my Lord and your Lord,
so worship Him. That is the straight path"

Surah Ali 'Imran 3:51

"Our Lord, forgive me and my parents and the believers the Day the account is established"

Surah Ibrahim 14:41

"And let there be from you a nation inviting to good, enjoining what is right and forbidding what is wrong, and those will be the successful"

Surah Ali 'Imran 3:104

"If the sea were ink for the words of my lord, the sea would surely be consumed before the words of my lord are exhausted"

Al-Kahf 18:109

"And He found you lost and guided [you]"

Surah Ad-Duhaa 93:7

"So be patient. Indeed, the promise of Allah is truth"

Surah Ar-Rum (30:60)

"And [remember] when your Lord proclaimed,
'If you are grateful, I will surely increase you [in favor];
but if you deny, indeed, 'My punishment is severe.'"

Surah Ibrahim 14:7

"It may be that you dislike a thing which is good for you and that you like a thing which is bad for you.
Allah knows but you do not know"

Surah Al-Baqarah 2:216

"Whoever does righteousness, male or female, while believing, we will grant them a happy life"

Surah An-Nahl (16:97)

"But they plans, and Allah plans.
And Allah is the best of planners "

Surah Ali 'Imran (3:54)

And say "My Lord, increase me in knowledge"
Surah Taha (20:114)

"The good deed and the bad deed are not the same.
Return evil with good "

Surat Fussilat (41:34)

"And hold firmly to the rope of Allah all together and do not become divided"

Surah Ali 'Imran (3:103)

And say: "My Lord, Increase Me In Knowledge"

Surah Taha (20:114)

"So let not this present life deceive you"

Surah Fatir (35:5)

"Allah (SWT) does not burden a soul beyond that it can bear"

Surah Baqarah (2:286)

"So verily, with the hardship, there is relief.
Verily, with the hardship, there is relief "

Surah al-Inshirah (94:5-6)

Made in the USA
Monee, IL
04 April 2022

94087376R00037